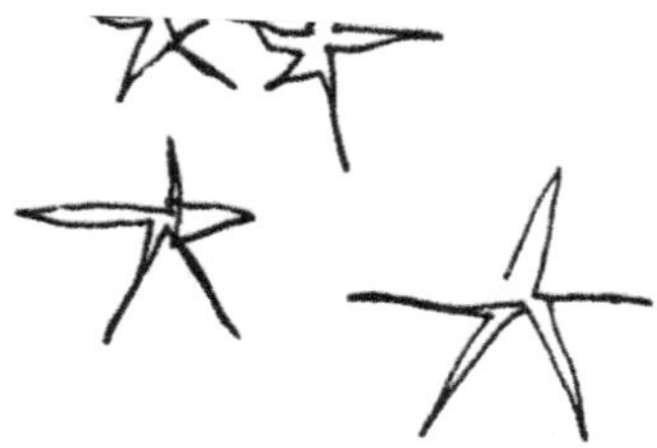

daddy's girl

by

isabelle cory

Cover designed by Isabelle Cory

Illustrations by Jamie KJ

ISBN: 978-1-915819-19-2

To my oldest friends, newest loves, and future desires.

OTHER TITLES BY IMPSPIRED

Fetch –
by Yvonne Hamilton

Stepping Up -
by DC Diamondopolous

Adele & Tom –
by Chella Courington

Curiosity -
by Geraldine Fleming

Incandescence –
by Mehreen Ahmed

The Babel of Human Travel –
by Maggie McKay

The Kingdom –
by Mary Farrell

A Snowfall in Paris –
by Theresa C. Gaynord

IMPSPIRED

preface

So… publishing a book. That feels like something I would never really get to do. It feels like one of those things that is just out of reach. Like winning an Oscar, or writing a dissertation (currently working on this one), or owning a car. It feels like something that I would never be asked to do. The idea that someone would reach out to me and ask me to produce a project like this one was totally not the plan. When Steve (Impspired) first emailed mentioning that he ran a small printing press alongside his magazine, I wasn't entirely sure what he was referring to. I thought he was just telling me for the sake of telling me a bit more about the business, but then I realised that he might be referring to my work specifically. Before I got too excited, I emailed back to confirm that that really was what he was saying and lo and behold, here we are!

A small warning before you get stuck into this one. This is not going to be plain sailing (nothing good ever is), there is a lot of hurt, so much uncertainty and quite a bit of swearing. But more importantly, there is unadulterated truth. There is looking yourself in the mirror and picking apart everything you see.

Then putting yourself back together again at the end. That's what this book feels like for me. It is an opportunity for me to lay it all out in the open, unafraid of what anyone might have to say about the honesty I have invested in. Unafraid of anything.

I want you to go into this book with an open heart and an open mind. You don't need to read it all, just the bits that speak most to you - keep those for yourself. My favourite way to experience poetry is to read it aloud, so maybe try that as well. Feel the words wrap around your voice and just talk for a while. To yourself, to those you love, to a room full of people. To keep everything locked away is to rob yourself of the chance to speak, to share and to connect with others. Language and communication is the only thing that keeps us all on a level ground, I encourage you to use it as much as possible.

Who knows what will happen after this project ends. Hopefully, another door will open and reveal something fabulous to me which I will grab with both hands. Whatever comes next, I am so proud of myself to have produced this book. I can only dream that you will enjoy reading it as much as I have enjoyed putting it together.

With love,

Isabelle x

contents

first year

A36
Twinings
Nine-forty-six
Take him by the hand
To my fife coastal town:
Petrol station macaroni pie
The monster under the bed

second year

Boase Avenue
I'm being irrational
Love letters to your voicemail
Stevie's lullaby
No hearts were broken
The angel of the lord

third year

Unhinged
Four day holiday
Piggybacking
The feminine urge
This way home
SADE SAID
The vultures
Shush
Wear your ring
Albany Place

fourth year

Readthrough
Things that happen on a monthly basis
Order up
Eatingsleepingwaking
Bedroom cogs
Detour to tayport
God is expensive & poetry is cheap
Jamie's song
Mushroom soup
Two little lines
Keep a toothbrush here

first year

A36

This room might as well be a graveyard
Time capsule of a place
Sucking out stale air
Filling in the gaps with grief
It's okay because university is supposed to be the best time of your life,

right?

Best time for nursing cough after cold with no sign of final sniff.

Best time for peeling skin until blood peeps sting pricks.

Best time for cradling her while she sleeps, worried she will choke on her own vomit.

Best time for asking multiple times for someone to leave.

Best time for crying when they eventually do.

If you held a light up to room A36
Who knows what you might find
Better almost to keep it in the dark
Better to be blind.

twinings

love changes the shape of the everyday things

a cup of green tea
a lazy morning spent in bed together

my t-shirt that you stained with coffee
the feeling of your arms

pancakes are not pancakes
they are your grumpy face as you admit that i am the best at making them

that song
i can't listen to it without thinking of –

i can't listen to it at all

i'm still picking off the hairs you left on my pillowcase
right now they are the remnants of our time together
soon they will just be a nuisance

soon the hurt will turn to an ache
and green tea will just be green tea

nine-forty-six

sitting backwards on a train

has the very physical feeling

of leaving everything behind

take him by the hand

make the boy a boat
teach him how to swim
how to breathe in
before the vessel pushes out
make the boy a song
teach him how to listen
how to let the music sing for herself
acknowledging every harmony
make the boy a heart
teach him how to hold it so
like as a bird fallen from the tree
learning how to fly again
make the boy a path
but teach him how to follow his own
how to get lost along the way
how to trust the sun and moon
make the boy a bridge
teach him that it's okay to cross
to walk away from the greener side
if the grass doesn't taste as sweet
make the boy a tear
teach him how to let others flow
how to accept the lump in his throat
how to let others know

to my fife coastal town:

your heritage hangs off my shoulders like a gown
sands stretch out from east to west
the pier meandering as far as the eye perceives

brunch happens all day in my bonny little town
tattie scones served with a steaming cup
and the sea brews just below the window

although me and my true love may never meet again
my feet still feel the trod of uneven cobbles
in dreams i sprint into your waters
in october, the early morning
when i close my eyes I am with you
sand holding tight my hands
ready for one last strip of the willow

petrol station	***macaroni pie***
Young with love	and an unweeded shame,
Smoke drifts through	the bedroom door.
She lays in sheets	under someone else's name.
Watched hands dropped	brings moth to a flame,
Always too little	(fiercely never more).
Young with love	and an unweeded shame.
Squared-up words	to plaster a rounded frame
Makes edges	and curves red raw sore.
She lays nameless	under someone else's sheets.
Rough handiwork	harvests her fresh terrain -
So deftly done	she can but watch and adore,
Young with love	and an unweeded shame.
Burnt-up breakfast	is sour, caked in blame
But like always,	blame fails to find who it's really for.
She lays in sheets	under someone else's name.
Easy to be disillusioned	with small-town fame,
	Put it down to luck of the draw.
Strung-up with love	and an unweeded shame
She lays in sheets	under someone else's name.

second year

Boase Avenue

Black mould infests this entire town
Speak to anyone and they will tell you
It crawls into every crevice and crack
Nestled in corners
Observing

Black mould has seen me cry
Countless times about the same thing
It's always about the same thing, isn't it?
Black mould has been there for every shitty essay mark
Every disappointing email
Every inspection
Black mould has seen me naked
Black mould has seen me naked after you took my clothes off
Black mould remembers how you never really asked for my permission
Black mould even saw the photo you took of me after we'd stopped
The photo that is now slotted into an album
Reminding me of all the memories I have
Black mould does not want to forget
And neither do I

After each time black mould just grew and grew
On the wall next to my bed
Walking into my lungs as I slept

There is so much gunk to scoop out from my body
So many things that aren't supposed to be there
Just like black mould,
It clings.
No-one seems to want to do anything about it
Not even me

i'm being irrational

i feel guilty about when the sun shines but i don't want to go outside
i feel guilty about not being able to sleep even though i've just closed my eyes
i feel guilty about feeling lonely because i know there are people i can call
i feel guilty for pursuing love because i know i will only fall
i feel guilty for singing even though i'm losing my voice
i feel guilty for being ungrateful when i know some others don't have a choice
i feel guilty for feeling trapped though there's nothing keeping me from being free
sometimes, i feel guilty just for being here, for wanting to be

love letters to your voicemail

when i get out of this place
i will run to you with arms stretched a mile wide
i will hold you as tight as the sand does the tide
praying that you never leave my side
i will capture your face in a thousand different ways
so that, no matter what,
i will always be able to find you within memory's maze
i'm sorry if i sometimes forget how hard i'm holding your hand
it's just the thought of being away from you again is one that i cannot stand
i've missed you, dear friend
time to make a new plan

stevie's lullaby

nobody knew her, the lost girl
only ever seen stroking the hair of a boy who spoke paper
promises of love
with her face turned away and a mouth full of lies, she lay
not listening, but having nothing to say

lonesome bird
when he'd asked if she wanted to fly
her wings stretched open wide
over time she saw that this freedom has its flaws
the cage that now kept her was never big enough to swoop or
soar

but the cage could be smaller
(still the boy's hair needed stroking)
so there she lay, obedient as a cuckoo clock
not listening, but having nothing to say

no hearts were broken

it was one night when they looked at each other
that they could almost fall in love
poetics never uttered
only shared heat in bedsheets
and at 2am they listened as their music played
'loving is easy' by rex orange county
she is tackled with a kiss
wrapped in a shirt of a boy that she knows
the boy's heavy head rests gently on her belly
in that moment, time is a scent that she could spray on her neck
she wonders what memory smells like
and now, looking in the mirror with no. 5 on her wrist
she wonders again
caught in a blink of breathless nostalgia
a still-life reflection
were it not for the salt that splits her cheek

the angel of the lord

so sweet a voice
if not for the poison lying dormant in your mouth
i feel it dripping down my throat
seeping into my hearts' veins
and just like a hand, it squeezes
my body is suddenly limp
your arms lift me onto the bed
for days i stay there
unable to talk, or sing, or breathe
i want to ask you to let me go

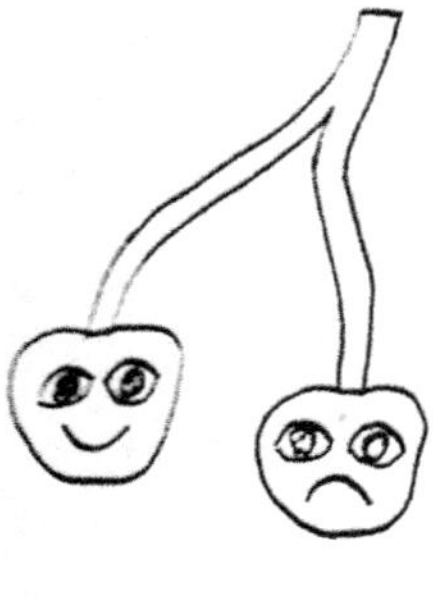

the monster under the bed

i dreamt about him last night
i dreamt that i told the whole world what he did
how his hands moved and touched
he didn't back down like i always thought he would
instead he stood at my front door
tried to get in any way he could
and when he did
he tried to kill me

third year

unhinged

thoughts of him yearn for my attention
like a mosquito bite that begs to be scratched
knowing full well that the itch won't subside

four day holiday

he probably thinks it's crazy
he's travelled all this way
visiting a girl he barely knows
but likes her all the same
with the hope of the uncorking of several bottles of wine
and fucking her clumsily on the sofa
instead he sees CRAZY
a depraved witch-type woman
using coping strategies for crimes she didn't commit
and dancing dismally in the courtyard
he's probably in disbelief
desperate to go home and resume his life as if nothing had
occurred
she will be here doing the same

piggybacking

in all honesty i was flying up awfully high
he must've thought it would be too much effort to pin her
down
and he's right
i should refer him to those who've tried

the feminine urge

to run away with someone
to elope
with someone not perfect, far from it
but is just here right now
to forget about everyone else
to never pick up the phone again
to drive and drive down roads well-travelled
to watch embers glow and seasons change
to dance
to swim in cold waters
to hold each other
to shout and scream into a waterfall
to share everything
to squeeze tight
to feel freedom for a second longer
to share the last biscuit
to hog the air bed
to burn yourself from the candle's wick
to bicker
to fight
to miss home and wish everything hadn't moved so fast
that feminine urge to push everything away
good or bad
to leave
to get your heart broken and double down in the sadness
to smother yourself in grief
pull the duvet up over your head
to not know why
to stop the movement
to go back to a place you've always known

and forget the person you thought you knew
to know that life is not a line you read in a book
to take leave
to be by yourself
to be yourself
to elope on your own
to tell no one about it
to keep a secret
and never tell a soul

this way home

is it bad that i still think about it
dancing boy
believe me i've tried not
you were so yearning
so proactive
even
coy boy
bury your head in the pillow with laughter again
ask all those questions again
answer mine not
gentle boy
gives me all the pillows
gives me coffee
and not a bite to eat
when can we share the same sun
or shelter from that same rain
the thought remains
farmer boy
let's feed the pigs
and watch them fly

SADE SAID

i remember his hands
and where they went
but i cannot recall my body
for the life of me
it ceases to exist in that particular memory
i've removed myself from the equation it seems

the vultures

do i gather them like mementos
like train tickets
and plane tickets
magnets
wristbands and nametags
or chewed up pieces of gum
these shirts from different boys i've known
scrunched up and tucked up into the closet and under the bed
someday i wonder if the memory will leak out of them
like blood that forms a pool under the wardrobe door
swimming across the floor climbing up into my bed
falling asleep next to me as if nothing's wrong
i'm in bed with it
sharing sheets with it
eating my mind up with the idea of it
let me wring it out of my bunches
wash it out of my mouth
take them all back
tick them off the list
ensure none are missed
i'm not a storage cupboard for the shit you should be taking to
your therapist
i'm sweeping you out
all your dust and mites and scraps and leaves
let me testify to the way you fright me
the way no one believed me
the way you still move freely
how can you still see me
see me
look at me here and tell me you did nothing wrong

shush

i started smoking when you decided to stop
and i regret you all the time.

you've grown so ugly these past few years
and i regret you all the time.

i wrote you a poem because i thought it would help
but i regret you all the time.

i went to therapy because i thought it would help
but i regret you all the time.

my mother said i was probably just regretful
and i regret you all the time.

i saw you as i rode the bus the other day.
i regret you all the time.

sometimes i find it hard to believe
i still regret you all the time.

i regret you all the time
though it's a waste of time to do it.
At least give me quiet
Let me move my own way through it.

wear your ring

keep telling me pretty words
water me and i'll grow
make lemonade out of me
string me together and wear me
hand-me-down
i am an heirloom
pass me and with no past be
treasure before and then forget
there will be music in us yet
forge us together
seal and solder us
never be bolder than us
thus,
give me your name and i'll give you mine
fear will never find me here
see and saw bounce me back to you
i thank the lord there's people out there like you

Albany Place

You cannot know this
But you did such a good job
Of keeping me safe

fourth year

Readthrough

I'm in a room full of posh wankers talking about posh wankers
Am I the only one who notices the irony
Am I the only one who notices
Fisherman's jumpers
Gucci belt and vintage booties
Chunky socks in faded three stripes
Surrey not sorry
Not too shabby
But definitely not too smart
Dressing up to look dressed down
A bouquet of buzzcuts and curtains
Booze bitch chap mate and fuckery
Lucky me

Things That Happen on a Monthly Basis

1)You become incredibly anxious about everything, it seems everyone is out to get you or at least annoy you.

2)Point 1 means that you do not want to do anything, and I mean ANYTHING. This includes: taking a shower, talking to friends, going outside, spending time with family, talking in general.

3)You develop a searing hatred for your mother. Everything she says makes you want to throw a chair across the room and fucking scream. The worst part is when she says that she "can't win" (this will 100% result in you storming off upstairs or to any other room in the house).

4)You become physically incapable of smiling.

5)You get emotional at the tiniest things. This could include: your crumpet burning in the toaster, spilling hot honey and lemon on yourself, not being able to know what to wear, your hair not looking good no matter how styles you try, and stubbing your toe.

6)You get emotional thinking about being emotional.

7)Your appetite revolves around two things: wine and chocolate. Lots and lots of chocolate.

8)You stare into space for a disgustingly large portion of the day and catch yourself in a trance almost every 5 minutes.

9)The thought of talking, even LOOKING at another person, induces vomit.

10)YOUR UTERUS LINING IS SHEDDING ITSELF AS A PUNISHMENT FOR NOT BEING PREGNANT.

11)Point 10 is an extremely painful process that cannot be explained with appropriate wording. It is not a stinging pain, nor an ache, it feels like thousands of gnomes are incessantly punching at the deepest pit of your stomach (whilst simultaneously hurling abuse at you).

12)PARACETAMOL DOES NOT WORK. Do not be fooled by Feminax either, she is a liar.

13)Hot water bottles are merely a plaster for what is a grossly large wound created from the bite of mother earth's shark.

14)DO NOT let anyone cross you during this trying time, they will not be prepared, and they certainly will not recover.

15)Bed is the safest place. Stock up with food and booze, you're gonna have to ride this one out.

16)You begin to think that you are clinically depressed or that you definitely have a diagnosable mental illness. The hard part comes a few days later when you look back and have to acknowledge that you are not mentally ill, you just have a uterus.

17)Hormones are fucking weird.

order up

i can feel my heart burning and blooming
like a fireflower in my chest
like indigestion if it was nice
like i've eaten you too quickly
refusing to wait in between mouthfuls
i'm at a lovebuffet and i'm going in for my fourth plate
i packed tupperware so i can take you home as well
i'm putting on groucho glasses so i can disguise myself as i go for
a fifth
i speak french to the buffet staff
i bring three different outfits
i am crafty and clever about you
i've paid a penny and i'm getting a million dollars' worth
this isn't even america
but boy, am i living the dream.

eatingsleepingwaking

two mugs sit on a windowsill
and no,
i don't just mean us
brushing hands with fake plants
and dead ones
there's ash in the coffee
coffee in the cigarettes
smoke billows out of the window
landing on air
as bombay bicycles ride around the bedroom
i feel eyes peeling away at me
i cannot bare the gaze between us
so i draw you onto the bed
sketching an arm around my waist
shading in your warmth
sunk into me as you fall back asleep
limbs heavy dreaming
day rises around like bathtub water
we breathe in the deep
floating up

bedroom cogs

this bleary-eyed
motherfunster

makes a slurring speech from his slumber

calling in sick to work again

the task is writ so he
slithers

down into this den we made

curling up to hibernate

until caffeine cracks his sleeping will

and bounding

down
stairs we go

the sun has got his hat on

his jacket and glasses too

we go outside along sands and t i d e s

bathing in

big deep blue

detour to tayport

you accidentally took the long bus
the one that you thought you always took
turns out there's more than one bus route
fortunately this scenic route is indeed
very scenic
instead of industrial estates
there's farmland
and cows
and grass
and mountains
you look across the mountains
with sunset sat behind
and think
this is one of those happy mistakes you sometimes make
trailing through town after town
you feel grateful for the journey
not thinking about how the journey will make you late to the
destination
thinking about it a bit
but the journey is surely worth it
you pass through a town that you know and wonder
shouldn't we have already stopped here at this time?
shake your head out of it
you like the journey
and you do not mind when you get to the destination
just as you are thinking this
you glance left
happy mistake turns into a simple one
there is a stranger walking up pavement
except this is no stranger
if only it was

the second you lock eyes you know him
you know it
you remember it
all of it
sprawled onto the back of your hand
you see it
it only takes a blink and there you are
standing at a bus stop in a 3-day old body with empty hands
he can see you
do you feel like crying?
do you even want to cry?
do you?
i don't know
i don't know that it feels real anymore.

god is expensive & poetry is cheap

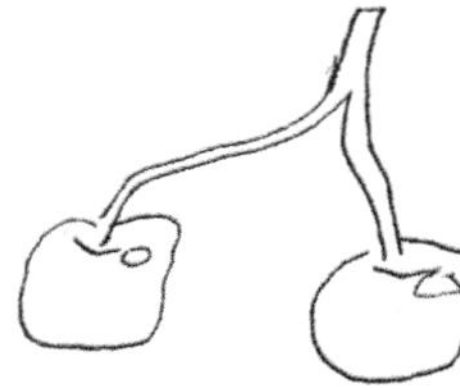

I always take more than one free sanitary product from the
public bathrooms in Scotland.
I don't wash my coffee cup if I'm having another one later in
the day.
I don't answer messages if they require me making a decision.
I don't like food shopping with other people because it makes
me cry in public.
I do not like crying in public.
I don't like paying for fuel.
And I hate when my flatmates ask me to give them lifts to places
that they could easily get to on their own.
I don't like it when my cat doesn't let me pick her up.
I don't like being rejected–
I don't like not having the hindsight to know when I'm about
to be rejected.
I want to be the one to reject.
I hate when people can't take a hint:
Like, just take the hint.
I hate men so much.
Not just one of them,
Or some of them,
But all of them.
I don't like how they've made me feel and continue to make me
feel.
I'm sick of their behaviour
I don't want to clean up their messes anymore.
I don't like having a shower and not washing my hair only to
realise afterwards that my hair could really do with a wash.
I hate that something like greasy hair can easily make me cry.
And I hate when I cry even when I don't want to.
Even worse, when I do want to, there are no tears left.

I don't like bad parties.
I hate when I'm conscious of my time being wasted.
I hate that i still feel shame about my body hair
even though it's my choice to grow it out.
I don't like having too much choice.
And I hate not having a choice to make.
Or having something chosen for you.
Another chooser's choice.
I dress up to make myself feel better,
To convince myself I'm not fat- that with the right outfit I can look desirable.
The trouble is I have nothing to wear (?)
I don't like how my bank account is in the minus.
And I hate that I'm the one who spent it.
I don't like the pressure of Christmas Day.
I hate that my favourite part is always unwrapping the presents.
I hate letting people down that I like;
That I trust.
I don't like not being the person that my parents thought I'd turn out to be.
I hate how my dad is never around to witness that for himself.
I hate how there's no clear answer for how to do life.
There's no guidebook or how-to video or a priest to tell me what to do.
And even if there was you know wouldn't be nearly as hot as the one in Fleabag.
Just some old guy in fancy dress,
Telling me to go on a walk and practice mindfulness.
Been there-
Done that-
Got the t-shirt-

to go alongside all the other shit I never want to wear.

Jamie's song

Today I'll pick you up, smooth you down and fold you
Slide you into the pocket of my hat
And I've finally figured out my favourite way to hold you

Formatted in italic – I'll underline and bold you
Sear you in heated salt-lick fat
Today I'll pick you up, smooth you down and fold you

The crafting market laid you out and sold you
Metal banding soft and soldered flat
And I've finally figured out my favourite way to hold you

The seasons' fast changing gives scares to cold you
Let me lend you my scarf and hat
Today I'll pick you up, smooth you down and fold you

Lush as carpet the world came and out-rolled you
Landed you here on my front doormat
And I've finally figured out my favourite way to hold you

It's nevermind that no-one ever really told you
"I'm here if you ever want to chat"
Today I'll pick you up, smooth you down and fold you
And I've finally figured out my favourite way to hold you

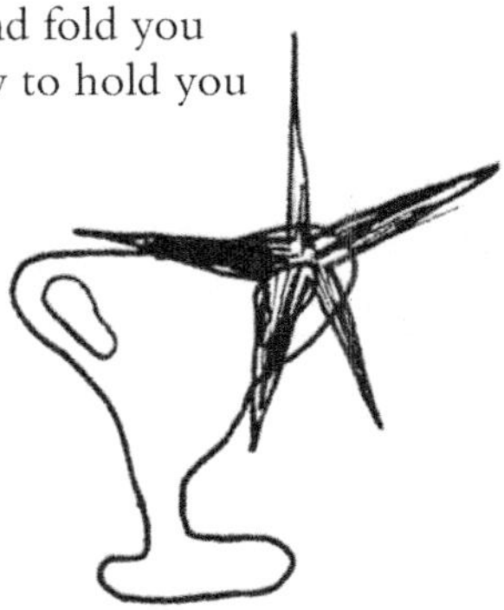

IS IT BAD THAT MY
CAT IS MY BEST FRIEND ?

mushroom soup

my mother probably screamed as i came into this world
and i can't seem to open my mouth now i'm in it
i wish silence wouldn't reign so much
taking all my words just to crumple up and bin it
paper trails to place in a dug-out grave
apart from the ones i never got to save
because i frightened myself out of proof
though it wasn't even me
frightened because this was a part of my life i really never
wanted anyone to see
sit me down just to tell me that it's bad
tell me that it's wrong
tell me i deserve better
ask me why i stayed for so long
and i don't have the answers for that
i don't have the reasons for that
from where i'm sat it's better to just ignore it
anything's better than admitting that
so don't tell me how to process this
how i should profess this so that everyone can hear my truth
and what this mess is
the bestest thing that i can do is what you see right now
here, in front of you
nothing more and nothing less, sis
nothing here to be tried or tested
this agony's been showered and dried
it's been fried
it's been well-rested
whether or not you decide it to be true
this weight
these words in the world of your palms

will follow you
and press you up against walls
bare-backed to brick and mortar
echoing down empty plastic halls
this cracked and brittle daughter
tell me now not to cry again and i'll do it
tell me to stand still and i'll have move through it
tell me to wait and i will never do it
bite me now, i'll remember the mark
memory pin-pointed as pricks
and laser fucking sharp
apart from the parts i can't ever seem to pick apart
but forget about that
like i always seem to do
for now i'll be the graceful girl my mother always knew
she'll give what's due and try to be proud
stand up at prize-giving and clap the most loud
ground me and hold me and sometimes stroke my hair
pretend she doesn't care about all the faults i'm yet to have
i'll take comfort in the way she says
"you get all of that from your dad"
in the end i don't know what this poem is supposed to be
some kind of daddy-issue therapy mix-up
(except without the fee)
keep listening because i will always have things to say
keep listening not because you have to
but because you want to stay

two little lines

I'm on a plane heading back to England. I can't help feeling like I'm returning to a crime scene. Like I'll look in the toilet and there will be something staring back at me. I feel so strange now that my body has returned to normality. All the time before I couldn't wait for it to be over so that the physical symptoms would pass. Now I feel like I'm coasting in neutral. Not feeling bad, but not feeling amazing either. What am I left with? What has this taken away from me? Anything? Have I gained anything that I lost temporarily? I feel vulnerable. Every year I get to this point and I feel lost. Again, this feeling of not being able to settle into gear. Unable to progress, not coming to a stop. I need to realign myself. I need to make myself feel comfortable. I need to be able to breathe. And focus. And deliver. And pull back. I need to give myself space and time and room. I look forward to the work I'll be undertaking this semester. But I also feel as though I am gearing up to something. Something big. Exciting, terrifying, unknown and right. Lots of big feelings going on right now. And time is flying by, so fast.

keep a toothbrush here

my muse is covered with music
stringing it together
you sing for me
bring breath into your lungs for me
play and shout and dance to me
sidestep away
and shimmy on back
into me
cradle yourself into the cavities of my body
sleeping your eyes shut
drifting away on the seas of my chest
and rest
dream our life to bits
with kisses and fits of laughter
spitting out pips
collect them and plant them in the pits
that litter our garden path

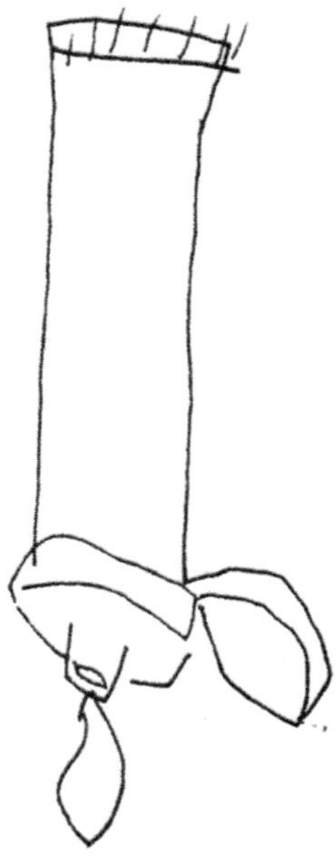

it is so dark when you sleep
i'm always leading up to weep
whenever you come around
your voice touches the ground
brows staying frowned
lay your head down
i said
it is early yet
neither bird nor worm have left their bed
lay your head
brush your breath against my shoulder blades
stay
be with me as though you do not want to leave
flee to another greener distance
picking
sticking yourself to some other noticeboard that people tear off

you are a paper person
with paper toes
paper ears
and a paper nose
paper eyes coloured with fountain pens
dripping ink stains on the pillowcase
dug out with a you-shaped dent

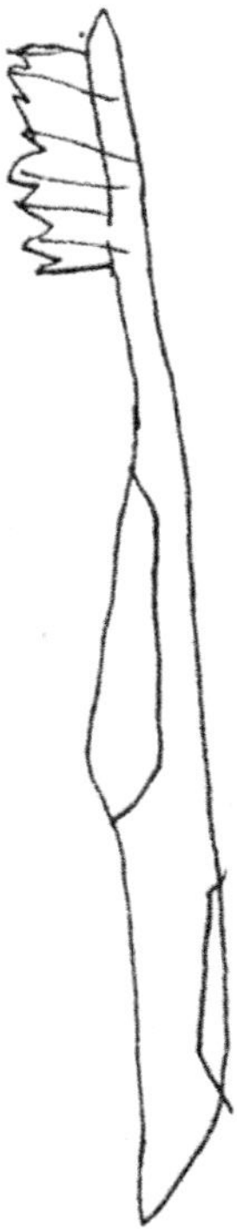

all my fire has been spent on you
every flame having went with you
bent and forged about your neck
hammered down
soldered into fleck
plunged into blistering water
and soaked heat
they have made a blacksmith out of you,
boy
spending days making solemn sparks
until you ignite me
rake the embers of my body
glove-less and beautiful still
to living ash
clashing together with metal tips
i am what keeps the house in bloom
at winter's knocking
when you beat the sun to rising
where weather bites
in stillness nights
i will thaw you
go door-to-door in singing
and adore you
before
and after
and now
and never
and always
and here
here in this so unimportant spot

with nothing to be in common
in fact so uncommon and rare

i stare back at the files of my mind
and kind of find what i do not find
is anything to bind this newer love of mine
this bewilderment-type love
shield love
to build love
filled by love
and eaten by love
small love
making loud love
to bedroom, love
and wash-up love
need love
i will come
to you, my love
come to you and let you gather up all my loose ends
i can pretend that i am made for you now, love
lend me your hands
knot them together in a bloodtie
and fingers fit to burst
will you never do your worst
chew on me or spit me out
you do not need to wash me when you've only worn me once
out
i promise i will last
months may pass
without you ever needing to ask
even when there are cracks in glass
that fracture the sun
this is more than father and son
so move on
and love others

love others
and you will be begun

acknowledgements

First off, thank you so much to Steve Cawte, the editor at Impspired. Without Steve, this book would never have came to be. He saw something in my work that was worth pursuing, and I'm so glad that he gave me the opportunity to do so. It has inspired me to believe that really anything is possible, you don't even have to reach for the stars to get where you want to be.

Thank you also to the wonderful people who inspire me in my life. To Eliza, who is one of my deepest, truest friends. She is now a part of my soul that I never want to shake off. Our friendship is the most steadfast I have ever known. To Sophia and Polly, my oldest friends, who have been my number one fans through everything I do. To Laura, my creative soulmate and co-founder of Turning Point Theatre

Co, I am so inspired by everything you do and I'm so grateful that I get to work with you. And to Jamie, and the wonderful love we share.

To my family, especially my Mum, who has supported me with every crazy idea I've ever had. She has watched me in dance shows, school plays, concerts, you name it. Mum, your love is priceless to me and I hope I never take it for granted.

Finally, to all of you who are reading this book. Thank you for taking the time to hear what I have to say, it means the world.

With love,

Isabelle x

about the author

Isabelle is a writer and theatre creative from Suffolk. She is about to complete a degree in English Literature at St Andrews University, where she has lived for the past four years. Turning Point Theatre Company was founded by herself and co-founder Laura Walker in 2022. They put on their own productions as well as using their creative guidance to develop scripts by emerging writers. Isabelle has written poetry for many years and began sharing her work on social media during the lockdown in 2020. She has since been published in two magazines, namely Impspired and Medusa, who have featured a number of her poems. 'Daddy's Girl' is Isabelle's writing debut.

Printed in Great Britain
by Amazon

21989910R00040